Travels in WESSEX

ANCIENT TRACKWAYS TO IRON ROADS

CONTENTS

WESSEX BOOKS

Ancient Wessex was a country of faith and magic and mysteries, and even today, once away from the noise, fumes and congestion of some urban blight, travellers can feel they move in the richness of an antique land.

The most famous and vivid legend of travellers of former days is that Jesus himself visited Glastonbury to dedicate the 'Old Church', and Blake's immortal words have still such a poignant immediacy that disparate English institutions adopt 'Jerusalem' as their anthem.

The New Testament tells us in Mark 15 that Joseph of Aramathea was granted leave by Pontius Pilate to take the body of Christ for burial in his own grave, and later monastic writings averred that at the instigation of Philip the Apostle he then journeyed through France and Wales to Glastonbury carrying the Holy Grail, accompanied by his son and ten others.

Of course, this early Glastonbury was an island in a Somerset yet to be reclaimed where early men had lived in lake villages above the waters, and journeyers would have had to cross water to reach it, but as far back as records take us, pilgrims have come to climb Wearyall Hill and the Tor and to wonder at the Chalice Well, and sites and relics now vanished.

But before Christ was born and before the Romans built their alien conquerors' iron hard straight roads, the prehistoric men of Wessex found the necessity to travel remarkably long distances, keeping mostly to the high

Joseph of Aramathea carrying the Christ child.

ground for their trackways above the tangles and dangers of woodland and scrub which reigned impenetrably in the valleys, as they journeyed to obtain materials for their primitive tools – flints for axeheads and knives and later in the Bronze and Iron Ages for metals, and for salt. Many trackways led naturally to the harbours and landing places of the South coast between Selsey and Portland Bill in addition to those which led to rich quarries and mines or embyro trading centres. Many of the high 'ridgeways' became supplemented by 'summerways' at a lower level when the upper courses of chalk streams dried up in the sunnier months.

A painting by A L Collins of the Ridgeway from The Icknield Way *by Edward Thomas.*

Several major trackways came close together in the Salisbury Plain including the Harroway, Lunway, the Lymington and the South Hants ridgeways. To the west of Salisbury what has been styled the 'Great Ridgeway' has a south–north course in its long journey from Seaton in Devon, passing Wayland's Smithy and the White Horse of Uffington, then south of Wantage and crossing the Thames at Streatley is part of perhaps the most ancient road in Europe and now under the supervision of Natural England is still a mecca for walkers and riders. Such is its singular importance it is now referred to simply as 'The Ridgeway'.

Despite the skills of science, archaeology and archive research there are grand uncertainties about our ancient ancestors' ways and means of physical communication.

Bottom right: Iron Age dug out boat.
Bottom left: The Glastonbury Lake Village excavations took place between 1892 and 1903. This picture was drawn for the Illustrated London News *in 1911.*

The great and mysterious constructions of Stonehenge and Avebury were part of the development that took place in Wessex after approximately 3000 BC. From AD 43, when the Romans arrived in Wessex, they began to construct their straight efficient imperial highways.

Rituals connected with Stone Age life consumed a plethora of exotic goods many of which had travelled vast distances. Of this period huge artefacts remain and we wonder at the technology (and tenacity!) which made the journeys for their construction possible. Stonehenge itself which was built, expanded and rebuilt over a period of 1,800 years incorporated bluestones from Wales which had been ferried, it is thought, up the Avon to Bristol, along the Frome, overland to the River Wylye at Warminster, along the river to Salisbury and the last two miles overland. Sarsen stones were probably from the Marlborough Downs 18 miles away, carried on sledges with wooden rollers hauled by a combination of men and animals. And all this carriage of hundreds of tons without the benefit of wheels, the knowledge of which had not yet reached our ancestors from its Middle Eastern origins.

Wessex was the land of the West Saxons. In this book Wessex is referred to both before and after the time of the Saxons.

In Wessex from Silchester capital of the local self-governing 'civitates' of the Atrebates, an important crossroad of routes, and Winchester the capital of the land of the Belgae, through Ilchester on the great Fosse Way which ran diagonally across England or Dorchester of the Durotriges to Exeter ran the roads over which marched the military cohorts who enforced obedience. The Romans had the horse and the wheel and a wide range of fairly crude carts and wagons, many obvious equivalents of the mail-coaches and carriers of the eighteenth and nineteenth centuries. Later oxen were preferred as draught animals for heavier vehicles undertaking shorter local journeys.

When the Roman Empire crumbled, Britain's island separation enabled it for a time to remain a secure and viable entity after Barbarian sword and fire had swept much of its Continental neighbours.

Below: *Portchester Castle.*

Inset: *Roman roads in Wessex, taken from* Romans in Wessex, *Wessex Books, 2008.*

Wessex developed into an energetic kingdom. Under the leadership of Alfred travel and trade began to burgeon using parts of the ancient trackways and Roman roads.

Eventually the Roman order of towns, country villas and farms linked by the great highways whose names we still know began to disintegrate in its isolation from the imperial power and culture. From the east over the sea came the predatory ships of the men from Frisia and Jutland and the shores of northern Europe. The Saxons came to us and over time Wessex (of the West Saxons) developed into an energetic kingdom with a new Christian culture; under the leadership of Alfred travel and trade began to burgeon once more, often using parts of the ancient trackways and former Roman roads.

Early Wessex had required witnesses for transactions in the countryside, for itinerant merchants were few in number but sufficient to require surveillance. Alfred insisted that traders should present their men before the king's reeve prior to departure to ensure their probity and good intentions. As they journeyed wayfarers were required to blow horns to alert communities to their presence. Some form of rudimentary wheeled vehicle was in use for Alfred himself. His preface to 'St Augustine's Soliloquies' instructs:

I advise each . . . to load his wagons with fair roads so he can plant many a fine wall and put up many a peerless building.'

Top left: A ship of the type King Alfred would have been familiar with.
Bottom left: Alfred's statue, Broadway, Winchester.
Below: Harnham Bridge, Salisbury. A medieval bridge widened in the eighteenth century.

Cartage and the maintenance of bridges were two obligations of service which the king could command.

Legend tells us that Alfred journeyed twice to Rome and certainly international trade and travel was ongoing, if slow and hazardous; Alfred's advisers John and Grimbald were Franks from the Continent and Asser, Alfred's biographer, spent time at Alfred's court and at St David's in West Wales from whence he came. Asser praised Alfred's generosity to travellers; Irish monks and a Scandinavian trader called Othere whose boats had journeyed as far as Lapland were among bene-ficiaries of his munificence. Of course, the king was not static himself in a 'capital'. A royal progress around the Saxon kingdom could involve stays at Cheddar, Portchester, Wantage, Old Windsor and many other places as well as time spent at Winchester, close to Hamwic (Southampton) the most sophisticated entrepot for commerce and industry.

Top right: Southampton Castle. A wooden keep rebuilt in stone in 1187. The drawing is from a contemporary plan.

Left: This gate led directly into Southampton Castle from the Castle Quay.

Below: Bradford-on-Avon bridge built in Norman time, a packhorse bridge widened in the seventeenth century.

From magnificent Venice which was the rich mistress of commerce with the East came ships and spices and mariners to the West country haven on the Avon.

From Roman occupation to the flamboyant progress of Tudor days, there is a sort of dark ages of transport and travel, and many of the more recognised histories of the times have no place in their indices for 'roads' or 'trade', England was growing to maturity and, despite the inhibiting character of many of its communications trade was developing. Waterway was frequently less hazardous than land travel and inland towns were often to a great extent ports on rivers. Bristol was early and independently prosperous not only reaching its mercantile fingers far and wide into the countryside but soon casting a covetous eye on the possibilities of foreign trade. One of those men, John Cabot, commissioned by Henry VII to discover unknown lands, arrived at Cape Breton Island on 24 June 1497, the first European to reach the North American mainland.

The Venetian, our countryman who went with a ship from Bristol . . . says that 700 leagues hence he discovered land, the territory of the Grand Cham . . . He is now at Bristol with his wife. Vast honour is paid to him; he dresses in silk and these English run after him like mad people . . . This discoverer of these places planted on his new found land a large cross with a flag of England and another of St Mark's . . .

Beaufort Tower and Ambulatory, St Cross, Winchester, which has continued to offer a wayfarer's dole to refresh travellers over the centuries, although now only a symbolic trifle. Painted by E W Hazelhurst.

In the Middle Ages new towns established themselves alongside the more venerable; of these 'new towns' Salisbury is a shining example. A product of ecclesiastical enterprise it arose when Richard Poore moved his cathedral from the water-short Old Sarum to its new site in the 1220s. Enclosed by a protective ditch and bank the cathedral occupied a major quarter eventually divided from the town by its own wall and gates. Salisbury flourished; a new bridge was built over the Avon, and the city became a hub for market and commerce with long spokes extending into a prosperous hinterland. It thrived whilst ancient foundations such as Winchester declined.

The replica of Cabot's 'Matthew'.

The Italian navigator, Giovanni Caboto (John Cabot), aboard the 'Matthew' in 1497. He disappeared on a second voyage in 1498.

'The Mayflower', 1620. The type of small Merchant Ship in which the Pilgrim Fathers sailed from Plymouth to New England in 1620. Displayed in the Science Museum, London.

The first few coach services established in the 1640s and 1650s could rarely guarantee any particular time-table as they were confronted with a myriad of potential problems of which mud, deep, tenacious gripping mud, was a universal treachery.

In the Middle Ages, there was nothing to match the brilliantly engineered roads of the Romans to make travel anything but an uncertain hazard. As late as the mid-seventeenth century the roads of Wessex were largely unmapped, including the important post road from London to Bristol; ways were not always clearly defined and journeyers often had unsignposted alternative diversions. From Hungerford westward through Froxfield and Savernake or on the drier hillsides north of the Kennet through Ramsbury to Marlborough were two such examples. A cross Samuel Pepys, that inquisitive diarist, lost his way between Reading and Newbury in 1668, seven years before Ogilby published the first map of these routes.

The following poster appearing in the late 1660s was a novelty and

The King's Head, Malmesbury by Cecil Aldin.

crowds turned out to see the first passengers who had committed themselves to Providence!

Each parish was required by statute enacted under the Tudors to appoint a surveyor of highways with power to call upon its inhabitants to provide six days labour with the necessary tools, carts and horses, without recompense. The supervisor had no training and the workmen were vehemently ill-disposed. Patchy toil with stones and muddy gravel was soon obliterated by passing traffic and the weather. Even royalty was not immune to the perils of travel, as late as the reign of Queen Anne. Defoe recorded:

On the NW of this city (Bath) up a very steep hill, the King's Down . . . the late Queen Anne was extremely frightened in going up, her coachman stopping to give the horses breath, and the coach wanting a dragstaff, run back in spite of all the coachman's skill; the horses not being brought to strain the harness again, or pull together for a good while, and the coach putting the guards behind it into the utmost confusion, till some of the servants setting their heads and shoulders to the wheels, stopped them by plain force.

Tempers were frayed, lives were lost and commerce was often risky and unprofitable where it was not downright impossible in these conditions.

Emmanuel Bow and John Owen in Britannia Depicta *1720.*

Turnpike gates were erected at which a toll was charged for passage for all except pedestrians, placing much of the burden of maintenance costs on to the heavy coaches, wagons and carts which broke up the surfaces.

To end this national disgrace and facilitate general progress the government introduced at the end of the seventeenth century a system of turnpikes for some of the most difficult sections of road; these were administered initially by justices of the peace. Eventually, a new type of highway authority came into being – the turnpike trust – a body headed by local gentry and professional men, in effect a private company empowered and required by parliament to exact tolls and repair particular stretches of road. It was all a bit piecemeal and it took about 50 years for the main Bristol road to be completely 'turnpiked' and about a dozen different trusts were involved in its upkeep. By the end of the eighteenth century trusts had been sensibly amalgamated to allow more efficient and co-ordinated operation of the principal transport arteries.

Knowing how motorists react to the minor irritation of speed cameras it will come as no surprise to learn that turnpikes continually produced bellicose and protracted disputes, and fraud and main force were endemic tribulations for the trustees. Stanley Harris in *The Coaching Age* described one altercation:

The Exeter Defiance, one of Mrs Anne Nelson's coaches from the Bull Inn, Aldgate, went through the gate at Staines; all the tolls at the gates below were paid by the guard every Monday, amounting to about £30. It so happened that the keeper of the gate near Ilchester had got in arrear with his payments to the trustees, and accordingly their clerk served a notice on the guard of the coach not to pay him any more tolls. The gatekeeper to counteract this move, shut the gate

Mail coach built by John Vidler, c.1797. National Postal Museum and Robert Blake.

Milestone to London.

before the time for the arrival of the coach. When the coach came in sight therefore, the guard blew his horn to no purpose, and couldn't get through till he had paid three shillings. Meanwhile with the assistance of a horse and trap, the pikekeeper reached the next toll, which the coach also found barred against it. This keeper being more obdurate than the other, the guard produced his tool-box with the object of breaking through the outwork. This led to fisticuffs between him and the keeper, in which the keeper came off best. The bout ending in the gate's being closed.

Nevertheless, improvements to the roads' construction had been limited. Watered from time to time to allay the intolerable dust, this liquid application served only to ensure more copious muck later, and still often dependent on involuntary parish labour as a work-force, things changed immensely for the better when the Scot MacAdam, himself for a while a road surveyor, invented a surface of broken granite bound together with slag or gravel, raised for drainage:

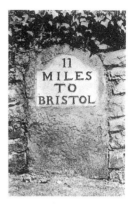

Milestone to Bristol.

They are perfection, sir,' says the proprietor. 'No horse walks a yard in this coach between London and Exeter, all trotting ground now.' 'But who has effected this improvement in your paving?' says Mirabel. 'A party of the name of M'Adam,' is the reply, 'but coachmen call him the Colossus of roads. Great things likewise have been done in cutting through hills and altering the course of roads; and it is no uncommon thing nowadays to see four horses trotting away merrily down-hill on that very ground where they were formerly seen walking up-hill.

Bath to London Mailcoach rushes by as the sack of mail is thrown out. Courtesy of the Communication Workers Union.

In their own words

John Evelyn, Diarist 1620-1706

We proceede to Salisbury:

So we came to Salisbury, and view'd the most considerable parts of that Citty, the Merket place, which together with most of the streetes are Watred by a quick current & pure streame, running through the middle of them, but are negligently kept, when with small charge they might be purged & rendred infinitely agreable, & that one of the sweetest Townes in Europe; but as 'tis now, the common buildings are despicable, & the streetes dirty.

We departed & dined at a ferme of my U. Hungerfords cald *Darneford magna*, situated in a Vally under the Plaine, most sweetly water'd. abounding in Trowts and all things else requisite, provisions exceeding cheape: They catch the Trouts by Speare in the night, whilst they come wondring at a light set in the sterne.

Samuel Pepys, Diarist 1633-1703

So came from Hungerford:

Where very good trouts, eels and crayfish dinner. A bad mean town. At dinner there, 12s. Thence set out wth a guide, who saw us to [Black Heath], and then left us, 3s. 6d. So all over the Plain by the sight of the steeple, the plain high and low, to Salsbury, by night; but before came to the town, I saw a great fortification, and there light, and to it and in it; and find it prodigious, so as to fright me to be in it all alone at that time of night, it being dark. I understand it since to be that that is called Old Sarum. Came to the town, George Inne, where lay in silk bed; and very good diet. To supper, then to bed.

And up, and W. H[ewer] and I up and down the town, and find it a very brave place with river go through every street; and a most capacious market-place. The city great, I think greater then Oxford. But the minster most admirable; as big, I think, and handsomer than Westmr., and a most large close about it, and houses for the officers thereof, and a fine palace for the Bp, and our guide, and I single to Stonehenge, over the plain and some prodigious great hills, even to fright us. Came thither, and find them as prodigious as any tales I ever heard of them, and worth going this journey to see. God knows what their use was.

The Plymouth Fly, from a drawing by Thomas Rowlandson.

Celia Fiennes was born 1662 in Newton Toney, Salisbury. She was robust, prim, but eager to see all that was new in a changing England – buildings, manufactures, agriculture – and she rode on horseback, often alone, at a time when the highways were in a deplorable condition.

The roads had actually deteriorated since the Middle Ages and the increase in wheeled traffic was making them worse. But wheels were still infrequent on the roads and carriage was almost always done by long strings of pack animals.

[FROM NEWTON TONEY its] 2 mile more to Stoneage [Stonehenge] that stands on Salsebury plaine – eminent for many battles being faught there, the many barrow or butts that are thick all over the plaine, and this of Stoneage, that is reckon'd one of the wonders of England how such prodigeous stones should be brought there; no such sort stone is seen in the country nearer then 20 mile; they are placed on the side of a hill in a rude iregullar form, two stones stands up and one laid on their tops with morteses into each other, and thus are severall in a round like a wall with spaces between, but some are fallen down to spoyle the order or breach in the temple – as some think it was in the heathen tymes: others thinke it the trophy of some victory wone by one Ambrosious, and thence the town by it has its name of Amsebury; there is severall rows of lesser stones within the others set up in the same forme, of 2 upright and one lies on the top like a gate way, how they were brought thither or whether they are a made stone is not resolved; they are very hard yet I have seen some of them scraped, the weather seemes not to penetrate them, to increase the wonder the story is that none can count them twice alike, they stand confused, and some single stones at a distance, but I have told them often and bring their number to 91.

Celia Fiennes, intrepid puritan, equestrian and recorder of change, 1662–1741

From Newton Toney to Salisbury:

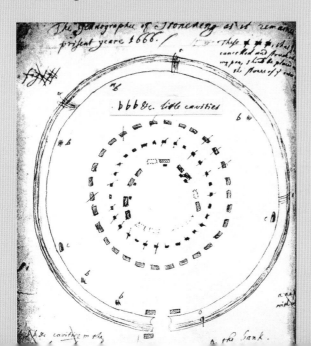

In 1666 John Aubrey spotted tell-tale surface markings around the stones at Stonehenge and labelled them as little cavities on this inaccurate but famous plan.

Despite the perils and privations of journeys prior to Tudor times the meandering unsurfaced roads between market towns or taking pilgrims to visit the many shrines were links that carried king and courtier, prelate and priest, merchant and moneyer as well as goods and information.

The image of the ancient inn, winter or summer, town or country has been used even by teetotallers as a snapshot of the best of England, a warm and hearty resting place unlike the bug-infested dens of ill-repute which lay in wait for Continental travellers: '. . . food and cheap entertainment after the guests own pleasure . . . humble attendance on passengers, yea even in very poor villages.' Thus Fynes Noryson an Elizabethan writer and traveller.

The inns had taken up the provision of bed and board which until the Reformation had been a busy function of many monasteries and religious establishments.

Glastonbury's tomb of Arthur and that of King Edward the Martyr at Shaftesbury were popular destinations for devotional pilgrimages. As early as the ninth century the name of St Edward was added to the deeds of Shaftesbury Abbey church and the town itself was known as Edwardstowe; the shrine became a lucrative source of income as the great faith and skilled nursing of the nuns did indeed work wonders for the fame of the Abbey and the prosperity of the town. For all this travel bridges were essential, maintained variously by bridge guilds, groups of parishes, 'hermits' who took the tolls and estate owners, by local religious houses or by charitable foundations.

Nevertheless many inns had been with us prior to the Reformation as Chaucer's tales so eloquently remind us. Literature from Chaucer to

Pilgrims pause to pray at stations like this one. Abbeys in Wessex drew pilgrims whose travels took them to Glastonbury, Shaftesbury, Winchester and other places. This prayer stone is in Glastonbury Abbey. The carriage is in the Dodington Carriage Museum, now closed.

Shakespeare and beyond has perhaps, on the whole, given us a picture of the better hostelries and more affluent travellers. Chaucer's host at the 'Tabard' was impressive and diplomatic:

'Bold of his speech and wise, and well-y-taught,
And of manhood him lackede right naught
        And saide . . .
        Now lordlings, trewely,
Ye been to me right hertely'
For by my trouth in that I shall not lie
I saw not this year so mirry a compaignye.'

And his travellers include Wessex folk – the Wife of Bath, the Shipman of Dartmouth and so on.

And even Falstaff and his crew, even if somewhat rapscallion were, off and on, drinking companions of their future king, Henry V.

'His companions unlettr'd, rude and shallow
His hours filled up with riots, banquets, sports,
And never noted in him any study.'

Chaucer's Wife of Bath from The Canterbury Tales, printed by William Caxton in 1484.

17

The virtues of the English hostelry as to comfort and convenience may have been extolled by many: 'But, alas, the willing servants and jolly host himself are often in league with the highwayman.' (Trevelyan). From the time that man started to travel some of his fellows have been ready to waylay and rob him. The footpad (on foot!) and the highwayman (on horse) reached the peak of recorded notoriety in the seventeenth and eighteenth centuries at the time when coach services became an organised and otherwise reliable and heavily utilised form of public transport.

The leading gentlemen of the road did receive some of the romantic adulation suggested by Alred Noyes' twentieth century poem *The Highwayman*:

Market Place, Reading, 1825.

'Look for me by moonlight,
Watch for me by moonlight,
I'll come to thee by moonlight, though hell should bar the way.'

MARKET PLACE, READING, 1823.

Canals and Inland Navigation

Waterways were from early times often safer and less obstructed passages for the transport of goods and people than land. Likewise the dragon prows of the longships of the Vikings could nose their way far up the estuaries and rivers of the Wessex coast. In medieval times the natural watercourses were crudely engineered in places (particularly by the great abbeys and monasteries) to adapt them for local transport. One example in the west is of the Somerset Axe which served famous Glastonbury. In the east the Itchen as far as Alresford enriched the ecclesiastics of the see of Winchester.

It was not until the eighteenth century that either substantially canalised rivers or newly created waterways came to form an extensive network to serve the burgeoning Industrial Revolution. Perhaps one should qualify the term 'network'; the word is reasonably appropriate for the east of Wessex where several large undertakings fed into the ancient highway of old Father Thames but in the west, in Somerset and Devon, the canals were more often short, separate and independent, despite

Waterways were from early times often safer and less obstructed passages than land for the transport of goods and people.

The Ferry Slip, Salcombe, Devon.

several more ambitious but abortive schemes to unite the Bristol and English Channels by a ship canal allowing a quiet passage for vessels otherwise forced to face the perils of rounding Lands End.

In Elizabeth's reign the Exeter Canal was opened south alongside the river Exe, partly to bypass an obstructive weir erected by a Countess of Devon who was anxious to give Topsham a monopoly of sea trade. In 1727 the Avon above Bristol was opened to Bath by the 'Proprietors of the Navigation between Bath and Hanham Mills' to be used by both passenger boats as well as commercial carriers.

From The Canals of South West England, *Charles Hadfield (David and Charles, 1967).*

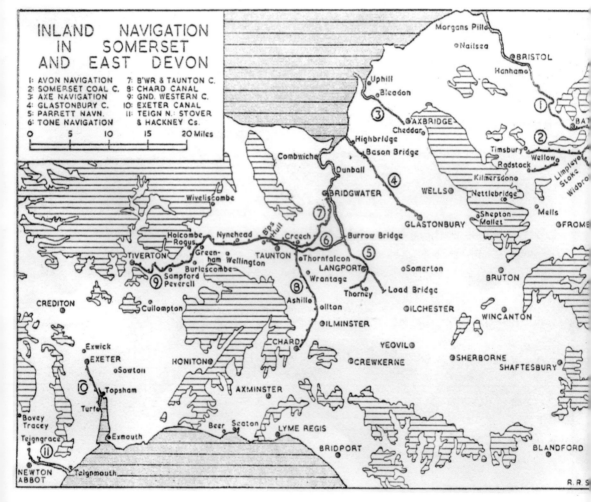

A Coach Goes into Portland

The great novelty of the day was the circumstance of a Stage Coach and four horses going into Portland. . . . Mr Gaulton, the landlord of the Antelope Inn at Dorchester, being determined to surprise the Portlanders, sent the 'Victoria' coach into the Island with the procession. Now persons need not feel the least timidity, as the island can be safely reached by land, without the necessity of crossing by boat. ANON.

Eighteenth-century view of the Ferry and Passage House at Portland, 1790.

The most substantial and still very much alive enterprise was the eighty five miles of the Kennet and Avon linking Reading with the Avon at Bath, and consequently allowing traffic to pass from the Thames to the Bristol Channel, but it was November 1810 before it could be reported:

We have the pleasure of stating that this morning for the first time a barge loaded with 40 tons of stone passed the locks from the river Avon to the Kennet and Avon Canal, near this city (Bath) and we are assured that 30 days working weather will so far complete the canal, that boats of 40 or 50 tons burthen may pass from London to Bristol without shifting.

Almost simultaneously, in 1810, was finally completed the Wilts and Berks Canal, another major project, leaving the Thames at Abingdon and running through Swindon to join the Kennet and Avon at Semington. Nine years later a further link was opened between the Wilts and Berks in Swindon and the older Thames and Severn near Cirencester.

By the time that in 1906 the government of the day set up a Royal Commission on the Canals in the light of their decline and

The route of the Kennet and Avon Canal.

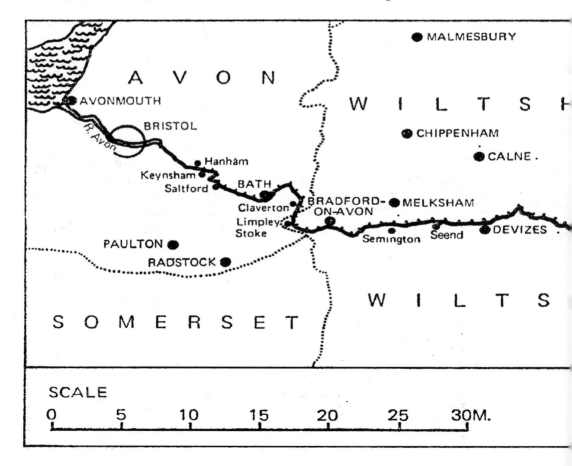

deterioration, the Wilts and Berks was already closed in all but name and the Thames and Severn largely derelict.

Our map shows us the various canals of the western peninsula. Most were opened between 1827 and 1847, for instance, the Bridgwater and Taunton in 1827, the Grand Western in 1838 and the Chard in 1842. Many were soon purchased and gobbled up by the railways, the Bridgwater and Taunton in 1866, the Grand Western in 1864 and the Chard in 1867. Fragments of these man-made waterways still remain, part of the Grand Western near Tiverton continues to provide tranquil passenger boat outings in summer.

The Somerset coalfield around Radstock was served by canals, they quickly succumbed to the railways and, indeed, the coalfield itself is rapidly becoming obscure history, the area's transport being prominently remembered most fondly by *The Titfield Thunderbolt*, a film (and latterly stage play), a comic tale of battles between train and bus shot on the long-abandoned Camerton to Limpley Stoke line.

The Act of 1796 for the Wilts and Berks Canal.

ANNO TRICESIMO SEXTO

Georgii III. Regis.

⁕⁕⁕

C A P. XLVII.

An Act for making a Navigable Canal from or near *Gain's Crofs,* in the Parifh of *Shillingfton Okeford,* in the County of *Dorfet,* to communicate with the *Kennet* and *Avon* Canal, at or near *Widbrook,* in the County of *Wilts,* and alfo a certain Navigable Branch from the intended Canal.

[24th *March* 1796.]

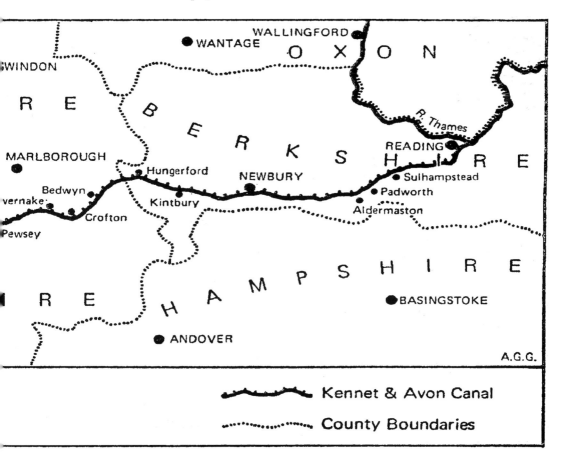

Kennet & Avon Canal

County Boundaries

It was not only that the exodus to the industrial cities had begun. Country towns had lost their economic base with the coming of the railways.

L&SWR London and Plymouth Express.

Thomas Hardy revived as a setting for his fiction the name of Wessex; Anthony Trollope invented a new county, Barsetshire, which was envisaged as a physical component of the same territory. Barsetshire was conceived on a warm evening in May 1853 in the Close of Salisbury Cathedral when as part of his endless travels for his employer the Post Office Anthony was engaged in the reorganisation of mail services in the south-west. As the man whose persistence ensured the provision of pillar boxes everywhere for the new penny post, he was in his writings often a meticulous recorder of travels by rail or rural cart. He was a great rider to hounds when opportunity allowed but the new inventions of the industrial revolution, particularly the steam engine, were causing a somewhat melancholy decline in aspects of rural life.

The coaching business was at its height when Anthony was a boy; stage coaches trundled, mail coaches (which also carried pasengers) bowled, and young men in the latest type of carriages raced all over the country on the smooth, newly-macadamised roads. There was traffic. The inns in the towns through which it passed enjoyed good and regular trade – feeding and stabling horses, providing meals and bed or an endless supply of travellers. Then the trains came, slicing through the countryside and carrying off the mails, and the passengers and the business. Anthony in the West Country witnessed and deplored, with many an "Alas!", the resulting stagnation.'

It was while I was engaged on *Barchester Towers* that I adopted a system of writing which for some years afterwards I found to be very serviceable to me. My time was greatly occupied in travelling, and the nature of my travelling was now changed. I could not any longer do it on horseback. Railroads afforded me my means of conveyance, and I found that I passed in railway carriages very many hours of my existence. Like others I used to read – though Carlyle has since told me that a man when travelling should not read but 'sit still and label his thoughts'. But if I intended to make a profitable business out of my writing, and at the same time to do my best for the Post Office, I must turn these hours to more account than I could do even by reading. I made for myself therefore a tablet and found after a few days' exercise that I could write as quickly in a railway carriage as I could at my desk. I worked with a pencil and what I wrote my wife copied afterwards. In this way was composed the greater part of *Barchester Towers* and of the novel which succeeded it, and much also of others subsequent to them. My only objection to the practice came from the appearance of literary ostentation to which I felt myself to be subject when going to work before four or five fellow passengers. But I got used to it as I had done to the amazement of the West Country farmers' wives when asking them after their letters.

An Autobiography ANTHONY TROLLOPE

Victorian Postbox.

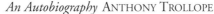

Original Bath Mail Coach.

Attack on Exeter Mail.

First Class Refreshment Room, GWR Swindon.

What it is easy to forget is that the coming of the iron horse spelt to a great extent the end of the glory days of our four-footed friends.

When the railway first came to Wessex it not only provided swift, accurately-timed communication enabling folk who had previously never explored more than eight or ten miles from their village to the nearest market, to consider bright lights and alternative employment of their country towns and, indeed, even to adventure in a fairly primitive steam-hauled railway carriage to the Great Wen itself, perchance to gaze incredulously at the wonders of the Great Exhibition of 1851 in Hyde Park.

The stagecoach gradually disappeared, the inn instead of bustling with the urgencies of travellers was the quiet resort of a handful of ageing locals; the saddler, the smith, the carter still had work to support agriculture and the farmer, but great lumbering steam machines for threshing and ploughing scarring the fields were auguries of their demise as well.

Hardy in *Desperate Remedies* paints a melancholy scene: 'The Three Tranter Inn, a many-gabled medieval building . . . standing on one of the great highways . . . had been in its time the scene . . . of much of what is now looked upon as the romantic and genial experience of stage coach travelling . . .'

'The railways have left you lonely here,' (Cytherea) observed . . . Save the withered old flies, which were quite tame from the solitude, not a being was in the house. Nobody seemed to have entered it since the last passenger had been called out to mount the last stage coach which had

'Tranquil Rose' at Caen Hill Locks, Kennet & Avon Canal Trust.

run by. "Yes, the Inn and I seem almost a pair of fossils," the farmer replied.'

Mr Toad of Toad Hall.

From Richard Trevithick's first little puffing machine trundling along the roads of the end of eighteenth century Cornwall, near to the opening of the First World War in 1914 there was a long hiatus of substantially deserted roads and increasing rural stagnation whilst the railway was king and before the internal combustion engine came to rule over us. One reads the many literary accounts of expeditions into the countryside, more often than not on foot, on lonely dusty highways of the South West, by writers such as Wilkie Collins and Edward Thomas. Perhaps it is only urban romantics who could refer to long tramps on the quartzy grit which was then a preferred road surface as 'a pristine majesty or Arcadianism at least'. Mr Toad in *Wind in the Willows* takes maybe a more utilitarian view of the matter as experienced in the upper Thames Valley:

> 'And to think that I never <u>knew</u> (the motor car)!' went on the Toad in a dreamy monotone. 'All those wasted years that lie behind me. I never knew, never even <u>dreamt</u>! But now – but now that I know, now that I fully realise! O what a flowery track lies spread before me henceforth! What dustclouds shall spring up behind me as I speed on my reckless way! What carts I shall fling carelessly in to the ditch in the wake of my magnificent onset! Horrid little carts – common carts – canary-coloured carts!'

Below: A steam train on the GWR main line westwards storms past the preserved Crofton Pumping Station which served the Kennet and Avon Canal which in the foreground parallels the railway.

Independent local initiatives brought the railway to Wessex, elements uniting until in the 1923 Grouping 'there remained two giants', the Great Western and Southern Railways. Competitive and clever publicists who until the Hitler war captured the sustained interest of boys of all ages.

When the railway came to Wessex in 1838 in the form of the first section of the Great Western Railway its primary aim was to link the city of London with the great port of Bristol. The countryside through which it passed was quietly rural, and travel was slow and mostly tedious. Even time itself was not standard but varied according to the distance west from the meridian, thus clocks in Bristol showed a difference of 10 minutes from those in London. The visionary engineer responsible for the Great Western Railway was Isambard Kingdom Brunel who rode hundreds of rain-soaked or sunburnt miles on horseback to the detriment of his health, planning his great achievement.

At the recent time of privatisation, Wessex Trains adopted the historic name for the services which it provided on a network of lines in Wessex itself, the West and part of Wales. The Wessex name has now disappeared as its Wessex operations are now subsumed into the First Great Western Group.

Further south again through Salisbury and Yeovil runs another east–west line, once the London and South Western and after amalgamation in 1923 part of the Southern Railway. Crossing these routes from north to south were less publicised routes, sometimes branches of the GWR and Southern. Sometimes to the delight of rail enthusiasts known as 'gricers' titulary independent and often highly individualistic companies – the Somerset and Dorset, the Midland and South Western Junction and the Didcot Newbury and Southampton, the majority of whose rails have long been ripped up and abandoned after closure, in common with so many of our much-loved but insufficiently used cross country rural railways.

Combe Row Station, fifty years ago looking north and showing the original engines on the West Somerset mineral railway.

One hundred and fifty years ago the Great Western and its associates' main line through Reading and Swindon to Bristol, Taunton, Exeter and Plymouth was up and running, but constructed to Brunel's preferred Broad (7'0") gauge, which had advantages over the 4'8½" largely adopted everywhere else but was a nightmare to co-ordination and co-operation. Its later conversion to conformity was expensive but rapidly achieved and essential for national 'progress'.

Another irritant eccentricity for the GWR was that it concluded a lease to the contractors building it for the refreshment rooms at Swindon; under which all trains were required to stop there for ten minutes. Apart from the impediment to swift running, the captive passengers complained bitterly of the quality of the fare offered. The GWR was unable to buy its way out of this nonsense until 1895. The great Brunel's letter to the proprietors has become famous:

'Dear Sir,

I assure you Mr Player was wrong in supposing that I thought you purchased inferior coffee. I thought I said to him I was surprised you should buy such bad roasted corn. I did not believe you had such a thing as coffee in the place; I am certain I never tasted any. I have long ceased to make complaints at Swindon. I avoid taking anything there when I can help it.

Yours faithfully
I K Brunel'

'The Cheltenham Flyer'. Engine No 5006 'Tregenna Castle' leaving Gloucester Station for its record breaking run on 6 June 1932.

A standard bodied Milnes-Daimler bus on a railway-promoted service at Avebury.

Thomas Hardy

Thomas Hardy, the writer who created a Wessex of the imagination using roughly the shires of the historical kingdom as his stage often sent his characters on long journeys, more often than not trudging wearily on foot through a countryside painted with hues of green melancholy.

Born at Higher Bockhampton, Dorset, on 2 June 1840, in his 88 years he was much on the move himself; in one year, 1875, he spent periods in Swanage and Yeovil as well as in London. In the next year he and his first wife, Emma, had their first home to themselves at Riverside Villa, Sturminster Newton. In 1881 he is resident in Wimborne, in 1882 in Shire Hall Lane, Dorchester, and in 1885 finally moves into the substantial Victorian edifice, Max Gate. Hardy was nearly all his life a robust if not physically over-ambitious walker and he was familiar as a cyclist in the Dorset streets, often accompanied by Emma clad in eyebrow-raising bloomers. His work is often threaded with railway scenes:

> 'A wee white spot of muslin fluff
> That down the diminishing platform bore
> Through hustling crowds of gentle and rough
> To the carriage door.'

For the motor car he was an early enthusiast, spending holidays from 1912 onwards touring the countryside in a hired car with his second young wife, Florence, and her aggressive dog 'Wessex' and driven by his chauffeur, Harold Voss.

Pannier Market, Barnstaple, North Devon.

A LONELY ROAD

At one place, on the skirts of Blackmoor Vale, where the bold brow of High-Stoy Hill is seen a mile or two ahead, the leaves lie so thick in autumn as to completely bury the track. The spot is lonely, and when the days are darkening the many gay charioteers now perished who have rolled along the way, the blistered soles that have trodden it, and the tears that have wetted it, return upon the mind of the loiterer.

The physiognomy of a deserted highway expresses solitude to a degree that is not reached by mere dales or downs, and bespeaks a tomb-like stillness more emphatic than that of glades and pools. The contrast of what is with what might be, probably accounts for this. To step, for instance, at the place under notice, from the edge of the plantation into the adjoining thoroughfare, and pause amid its emptiness for a moment, was to exchange by the act of a single stride the simple absence of human companionship for an incubus of the forlorn.

Below left: Thomas Hardy.
Below right: Stonehenge Rail Ticket.

The Woodlanders THOMAS HARDY

The Roman Road

The Roman road runs straight and large
As the pale parting-line in hair
Across the heath. And thoughtful men
Contrast its days of Now and Then,
And delve, and measure, and compare;

Visioning on the vacant air
Helmed legionaries, who proudly rear
The Eagle, as they pace again.

The Roman Road.

Further Reading

It would be presumptuous (and impossible) to provide a bibliography here. Wessex has enriched us with an amazing treasury of literature and among those who could not find a place in our text and who travelled our roads are Jane Austen, loved by all the world; William Barnes, the poet of dialect and Dorset; William Cobbett, the 'noble agitator'; Daniel Defoe, who fought with Monmouth at Sedgemoor and on and on . . . serendipity will take the reader into further delights.

Acknowledgements

page 2 left, Pitkin
page 4, Kay Ainsworth
page 9 top, Godrevy Publications

First published in the United Kingdom in 2012 by Wessex Books
Text © Douglas Stuckey 2012
Design and layout © Wessex Books 2012
Illustrations by Matthew Harvey
Cover artwork by KFD Ltd

Edited by Jane Drake
Wessex Books, 10 Thistlebarrow Road, Salisbury Wilts SP1 3RU
Tel: 01722 349695
Email: info@wessexbooks.co.uk
www.wessexbooks,co,uk

Printed in India

ISBN 978-1-903035-39-9

Wessex takes wings and goes international. Samuel Franklin Cody with Amerindian friend at Farnborough, Hants, Crown Copyright 1908.